THE TWO-HEADED
MAN AND THE
PAPER LIFE

Anatoly Kudryavitsky

MADHAT PRESS
CHESHIRE, MASSACHUSETTS

MadHat Press
MadHat Incorporated
PO Box 422, Cheshire, MA 01225

The Library of Congress has assigned
this edition a Control Number of
2019901980

ISBN 978-1-941196-87-8 (paperback)

Cover art by Marc Vincenz
Cover design by Marc Vincenz
Book design by MadHat Press

www.MadHat-Press.com

First Printing

To Yulia
my daughter

TABLE OF CONTENTS

Part I. The Memory Shop

Part II. Cryptomeron

Part V. From "An Uneasy Habitat"
Versions by Carol Rumens

PART I.
THE MEMORY SHOP

The Wind of History

The beggar was standing in the underpass in front of the Ministry of Education. Noticing a rare passerby, he unbuttoned his Commissar greatcoat with the suddenness of a magician's gesture. The art of the future, which he heralded for quite some time, instantly came to light from the pockets full of poets, musicians and actors. Having pulled out one of those figures, he began to inflate it with puffs of vain air.

No one was paying him any attention; they all were going on about their business. Deeper into the night, a couple of culturally concerned passersby pitched the idea of inflating all the figures at once.

The clock finally struck midnight. The figures were staring at the concert and theatre playbills and bowing like puppets in the wind.

Somewhere in Eastern Europe

It was the year the townsfolk shaved off their hair, believing that bad thoughts were getting trapped in it. The hairstylists were banned from the area. The gray-winged hens of Palawy laid their eggs all around the town.

After school, I worked my way home through hair-drifts. My grandmother acquired the strange habit of tearing away the last page of my school compositions. She assured me that one day I would understand why.

My grandfather often said that she intended to tear away the last page of his life. He left her and started floundering through the side streets of women's hair. Unhatched chickens laughed at him from inside their speckled eggshells.

I was advised not to mention my parents either at school or at home.

"You'll learn to forget," my teacher comforted me. "You'll live a good life."

In a Whale's Belly

The happiest years of Jonah's life were the ones he spent in the belly of a whale. He didn't have to strive toward anything, simply because there was nothing to strive toward. He didn't even have to feed himself, as the whale's stomach supplied Jonah's organism with a perfect combination of nutrients and ideas. Of course, it was stuffy in there, and it smelt fishy, but in general Jonah found his situation quite bearable. In those times he loved to talk about the lengthy and mutually profitable coexistence of mind and matter, i.e., of a man and the outer world. Even so, he was aware of the fact that neither time nor the outer world exists in the belly of a state-wide mammal.

One day Jonah got an idea in his head: namely, that of freedom. He prayed unto the Lord his God for deliverance, and so the whale was instructed to spit him up on dry land, which proved to be a lot drier than he had expected.

Before too long Jonah grew remorseful about getting out of the whale. He felt sorry for himself, and spoke to the other swallowed-and-disgorged, always moaning about not living a proper life. He even began to search for another whale interested in swallowing him up. However, the whales were not in any particular hurry to let him into their interiors; they drenched him with some of the water that had been processed inside them, and waved him off with their massive fins.

5

The Book of Meros

A papyrus recently found in the Desert of the Unthinkable stripped the profession of chronicler of all the covers of sense. At the very top of the scroll a few words can be seen set down in very shaky handwriting: "The Book of Meros." This is believed to be the title of the manuscript. Down the endless, glossy coils riders gallop, chariots whirl, swords clink, buildings collapse. No one sits there making sense of a past.

The roll absorbs everything that has happened since the dawn of creation up to the movable "now." With each passing day "The Book of Meros" gets longer, but the memory of generations gets shorter. The course of events will soon catch up with the flow of time, and then, possibly, overtake it. Maybe this means that we shall read in the mornings of what we are destined to do throughout the day—who knows? What we shall do after we find out what we are to do: that is the question.

Virgo et Leo

for Alex Bramwell

In the sandy well of the arena under the blue hemisphere of thrill, her nakedness manifested itself stronger than her guilt. A lion emerged, roaring, from the cave of all fears; his eyes, jewels of a greedy merchant; his paws, cedars of Mesopotamia.

Sunburst ... Orange puddle water ... The realm of opportunity was all aglow....

Then the air snapped in half, like a twig. The beast lay down at her quivering feet; he was protecting a cub, and the cub was she. As the crowd's disappointment was flapping its giant wings, the locks of time opened for them and mountains breathed out the chill on their faces.

Even these days her cringing lust for him is still alive, although he now is a stone lion in Nottingham and she a forget-me-not in the nearby garden.

The wind of late wisdom croons us a simple melody: "We love what tries but fails to kill us."

Visitors' Book

In the maze of my inner vision, there's a guest at the threshold; he wears the painted mask of a culture-bearer.

I ask him inside. He plonks himself down in a chair that resembles an antique lectern; his plumage trembling.

"I am Visitors' Book," he whispers haltingly. "People engrave their words in my skin." He is sporting a dagger tattoo. "Repeat three times after me: *the viola has fallen into the sea*.... Does it create an image in your mind, or have your blazing wells run dry?"

I offer him a glass of claret. "Weak ink," he mumbles after taking a sip. The open mouth mask covers his ears. "Now, get on with it. Write briefly; give it only a slight press. Every touch leaves its trace."

I am being careful not to use sharp instruments, but there's blood on my fingers and the inscription is illegible.

The Oppressive Lightness of the Void

Mr. Nihil is an every-parade's balloon. Watch his *Drang nach Westen* as he sails into the pub and orders tea, his warhead aimed at the world map underneath a little Statue of Liberty.

"Europe is shrinking, but America is broadening. We'll all be Yanks soon," he drops a few verbal bombs. "Not only are forms not expedient but they also outlive ideas. Where would Caliban be if he stopped fighting the Taliban?"

Mr. Nihil likes playing the game where one becomes the Roman dictator. He read somewhere that life force and inspiration are always at the other end of the Celtic spiral, especially since this kind of spiral is endless.

Europe in the mirror of his teapot is hard to recognize: the silvery curve enlarges France and Germany but lessens other states. The gaps between capes and islands are mended as if an invisible giant has put in stitches. Sipping his oil-tasting tea, Mr. Nihil searches for the meaning in this image of unity and distortion and also in their strange synchronicity.

Sex Toy Mistaken for an Angel

As the morning opened its folds to sun pillars, the islanders went scavenging among exiled chairs and floating doors— and she presented herself prettily, slightly sluttily, her lips seemingly ready to French-kiss the rose of Creation.

They knew nothing about the adult paraphernalia but felt certain what the aspect of an angel should look like. Don't we all?

When they grabbed her, she unloosed a full-body hug and faltered. They found her as worshipable as the moth-bird goddess or the webbed fingers of dawn.

What was pulsating inside police pencils? Which invisible cauldron belched out a chill in such an Arctic manner? Positioned by a crack in the cell wall that bleeds yellow rains, the doll has since been staring into heaven through a gap in the thick crochet of clouds.

And the islanders have reverted to revering the Unseeable.

A Promenade

Setting off for a walk into town, Professor Tausendteufel puts on his blind spectacles, takes his flowering walking stick and adjusts the angle of his body's droop. The correct angle has to be forty-five degrees minus the current temperature of the air.

The professor subsists on odors. Since professors and odors feel at home in the city, he enjoys the promenade and smells every sunflower and cow-dropping. He spends a considerable amount of time in front of pigsties. Not that he feasts his eyes on pigs, not at all, but he clearly enjoys their adoring looks.

As soon as the squeaking of mill wheels reaches his ears, he directs his steps into the heart of the city. Watch him stand in the middle of the central square and sniff at the fresh azure of cornflowers; watch the man who resolves, by the mere fact that he exists, all the contradictions of our illogical world.

Fathering an Island

If you father an island, make sure it's an ample child—Borneo, anyone? You like to think that you'll always be comforted by some tropical sounds awakened inside hushed oblivion.

If you father Great Britain ... but why would you want to do that? Besides, one can only queenmother it, and that position has long been filled.

How about Greenland, where the Moon's hollow mare swallows lower stars? Probably not a very good idea. Maybe Crete, with its shadows of the Argonauts and the Bronze Man? Sounds exciting, especially if you can dream in Greek.

What else? Hawaii, where each wind-arcane promise is a necklace on a cactus? Elba, where a lucid libertarian becomes less and less of his former self?

At first light, the ink of the sky dissolves in your clouded eyes and you realize that what you actually father is a rocky cliff surrounded by icy water. You can't land there; you can only admire it from afar and photograph it for your wallpaper.

The Worm of Doubt

In the spacious classroom of reason things learn to reveal their self-concepts and make themselves useful. While back-bench snakes eat their way forward through the rows of unsuspecting frogs, the worm of doubt thins the convolutions of pliable brains and subsists on forbidden fruit from the school garden.

In the meantime, the sky blossoms with interrogation marks and elusive smiles. The heavenly dictionary sheds weighty words, and they batter the garden. People disassemble them and build language barriers. Surrounded by walls and thorny hedges, things take the exam for the right to be called things.

Soon the breeze wafts a whisper from inside: "Pity stands the test: pity is always pity. Love will have to take a re-examination."

The worm wriggles, convulsed with the sense of having done his duty.

PART II.
CRYPTOMERON

Witness to an Underwater Time

Not many people might have noticed that the octopus, apart from having eight legs, also sports a tie. The octopus doesn't seem to be able to elucidate why he needs such an adornment of his outfit—can it be a sign of his confidence shaken too often? Generally speaking, the octopus is honest, meticulous and not particularly well-off. He doesn't need a lot. Comprehending the infiniteness of the underwater trails on which his era lost its way, he directs his mind toward himself: "I am a creature with no name or biography. I have a body, but it's almost translucent. My brain is completely see-through. My memories are gradually fading; my voice cannot be heard from under a bushel. So what's left? What's left?"

The sharks give wry smiles: there's plenty left: ink.

Agamemnon in Cambridge

Agamemnon is Lecturer in Psychology. "You love someone when you don't know him, and you know someone when you hate him," he says.

"And knowledge transforms your face, so when you reach forty you receive ambiguous greetings from the mirror," adds somebody's portrait from the wall.

After the lecture Agamemnon proceeds to the bar and drinks goats' milk. The milk is delivered specifically for him from an Irish farm.

"Is private life important for a male scholar?" one of his students enquires.

Choking on his milk, Agamemnon thinks that he would love to send the hellion to Hades for such a smutty innuendo, but he responds aloud, coolly: "A man can live in the heavenly pastures too. Oh yes, and he can fantasize about the love of women and all people. The clouds will show him such love, and even rather figuratively—unveiling to him three noble visions."

Nostalgia

One hundred and fifty years after his last visit, Gogol returned to Italy—this time under the name Tarkovsky. Every now and again dodging scooters, he walked around the Palatine and then unexpectedly found himself at the tomb of Roman literature. The tomb gave him a scare: he disliked tombs, literature and even Rome itself.

He winced painfully, and went back to his hotel. While getting the key at the reception, he noticed that he was again being reflected in other people's mirrors. His chin looked familiar, Gogol thought, but his lips were speaking in a tongue he didn't really understand. What were they saying? That man is easily translatable into another language, but who will be willing to read him?

In the evening, he sharpened the swan quill that he found in a public park, and used flame-colored ink to write the following in his diary: "He who reads not what I've written, but me, derives a strange pleasure from this. Otherwise he wouldn't entertain himself with this for such a long time. In fact, he could slam the book shut without embroiling himself in any moral implications. I, too, can slam myself shut, but I don't do it because of my professional habit of reading two-volume novels to the end and watching two-part films until they send me fast asleep."

Pabako

The pabako is an exotic fruit. It doesn't grow everywhere, and one can even say that it doesn't grow anywhere, but still it is being imported from some remote place, put onto tables— and people realize that it's edible, much to their delight. So the pabako would almost be the fruit of people's minds, were it not for its juicy blue flesh under the snow-white skin. It also has a red fruit-stalk, and so the pabaco tree is regarded as sacred in the countries with red, white and blue flags. Since countries like this are plentiful, the pabaco fruit is considered a national dish in each of them.

Most people have purchased packages of pabako juice, which makes the skin white, eyes blue, and brings to the cheeks the so-called bashful blush of a pabako-eater. But even half-liter juice cartons are so expensive that people only buy them during monthly national holidays. They say it is better this way, because a more frequent consumption of the juice— or the compote made of sliced white and blue pulp and soft, crispy red fruit-stalks—affects people in a different way: their skin turns blue, or even indigo, eyes become red and hair snow-white. Such people, like ancient prophets, evoke holy horror in the ones they meet; people steer clear of them and leave for them the most unpleasant task: fervently caring about their blue, white and red homeland. These gray-haired, blue-skinned individuals with bloodshot eyes keep out of sight; they are taken around in vehicles with tinted windows and live in houses where the windows are non-transparent.

In a certain country the pabako fruit has even ended up on the national flag, next to three lions, which for many years have been baring their teeth at it, incapable of taking a bite. This flag is meant to demonstrate the impossibility of achieving complete human happiness, which the inhabitants of the white, blue and red country had guessed long before the flag was adopted.

Were you to ask the author of these notes whether he had ever tasted this extraordinary fruit, he would give a positive answer. If truth be told, he belongs to the so-called chosen ones who are permitted to write about such sublime matters as the sacred pabako tree, the monthly national holidays and being zealous about one's native land. The chosen ones write on white paper with red ink, and sometimes even with the blue liquid that runs through their veins.

The Polish Corridor

Marching across Europe, Napoleon unexpectedly ended up in the Polish Corridor. This corridor was decorated with horned Teutonic heads and the coats of arms of the Polish gentry. Napoleon was moving toward the Baltic, but somehow kept finding himself in Eastern Prussia. The Russians were getting there, too; for courage they fired slingshots at Napoleon, and then promptly ran to hide in the Livonian swamps. Reloading the slingshots, they exclaimed: "May peace prevail on Earth!" Napoleon stubbornly went forward and, scratching the wool on his back, thought *I'll teach you a lesson about peace you won't soon forget!*

At last the pebbles ceased tickling his back. Napoleon was about to revel in delight when he realized that he had unwittingly wandered into a peaceful future. He turned around, but failed to find a single one of his soldiers behind him.

When Napoleon eventually escaped from the Polish Corridor, he found his way back into the past and, cross as a bear, set sail willingly for the island of St. Helena to make the whole of Europe shudder.

British Lions

When lions began to speak English, animal-keepers were the only ones who could understand them. Others didn't take the whole thing seriously: Wittgenstein famously said that if lions could talk, they would stop being lions. He didn't clarify, however, if animal-keepers would remain human, should they understand lions' roaring.

On Sundays animal-keepers and lions sit up straight at the round table in the local inn and, scarcely exchanging remarks, divide between them a huge Union Jack cake.

The Remote Control

In one of the shadowy worlds created by the general's post-television clear night vision, the parliament finally entrusted to him the remote control of his dignified self.

"Too late!" exclaimed the general who was left wondering what to do with the remote: in the past he was controlled by the fiendish state, which he, in his turn, later governed. However, with his low energy, there was no chance to control anybody any longer—or even to really influence the future.

The general was sitting in a shady backyard patio eyeing a Che Guevara poster and switching back and forth from channel to channel until his second wife seized the remote from him. Before long it found its way to his third wife, so young she could have been his granddaughter.

Non-Convertible Yuan

All fall silent as Non-Convertible Yuan arrives in the marketplace. Trade comes to a halt. Bells ring. Peasants bow obsequiously, and cross themselves in a Buddhist manner. While the inflated face of Give-Me, the chief party-line setter, soars above the rustling clouds, Non-Convertible Yuan walks around the counters flashing sunny smiles at women and displaying the metal of his muscles. He knows that before long he'll have to quit the scene, but he also knows that he will later make a comeback—in another country, under a different name.

Anatoly Kudryavitsky

The Peculiarities of Vision

It was the year the Short-Sighted declared war on the Far-Sighted. In the besieged capital of the latter, unread books flapped the wings of their bindings, hopping from roof to roof. Interrogation marks pranced up and down the streets like seahorses, each wearing a waist belt and a saber.

On the heavily rutted path leading out of the city I met the missing children whose snapshots I had seen in a morning paper. They were coming in the opposite direction, one by one. A bespectacled, almost pellucid teenage girl asked me if I was sure I was going the right way.

Hunting in a Flagged Zone

for Gail Hazelton

When you kill wolves, some people die. It is always the case. They bury the corpses together with the wolves.

Years after they exhume them, and re-bury them wrapped in flags. Each time they take the flags from the living.

The latter squat and cry a lot, naked, shielding with both hands not what naked people usually shield but spots of wild grayish wolf skin on their breasts and withers.

Economy

The supervising surgeon stepped out of his shadow, a trickle of seconds cooling his neck. He turned on white electricity, found a seat in the corner of the round room, and sent a neon smile in his patient's direction. "With you being Professor of Geography, we certainly won't lose our way."

The professor reluctantly began to saw off his spare leg. The operating theatre's glass eyes were watching, sprinklingly.

"What were you feeling at the bloodletting moment?" the surgeon asked the standalone leg. The latter, properly anaesthetized, felt nothing, and so began to ponder what the God of Economy would experience in this situation.

Having received no response, the surgeon hid himself in black embarrassment while the professor, now two-legged, studied the geography of the saw cut reflected in the mirror ceiling.

Call of the Abyss

Night was floating down the black river from town to town, from century to century. History trailed behind, snorting and spitting out mud. At some point in space an unplanned stop occurred, and out of the timeless quietude the words came out: "Fare you well, Ramirez, Gonzalez and Rodriguez. The Abyss is calling you!" This was followed by an abrupt command—and a splash....

A general materialized out of the primeval dark, and was quick to announce where the next unplanned stop would be. Three shiny gold medals with images of Ramirez, Gonzalez and Rodriguez jangled mysteriously on the general's uniform. The darkness did what it does best: closed in.

Part III.
The School
for Slow Reading

Gravitation

A ceiling gravitates toward the floor. Only transparent larch-trees, able to breathe in a closed space, though invisible, can hold it up. The ceiling lies on their tops, and creaks, and groans in frustration.

The floor, however, is by no means drawn to the ceiling. Quite the contrary; it gravitates toward Mother Earth who never strives for anything but rolls like a ball from footballer to footballer, from kick to kick.

The Sky in their Eyes

"A thin crescent of the waxing moon can be used for chopping up vegetables," a sky watcher made an idle remark. "For mowing lawns one has to employ a crescent of the waning moon," another muttered.

Later that day, giving an extensive celestial map a wandering look, they chanced upon the point of warmth. A certain small register suggested to them an idea as to why their eyes were warm there. On each page of that register there was dusty debris of a heavenly body hit by a well-aimed meteorite, except for one page, on which a newborn Sun smiled a happy smile, seemingly not even suspecting that there's no void without silent stones, whizzing.

The Three Fishes Theory

There are people who sincerely believe that the Earth rests upon three fishes: a pike, a carp and a flounder. If you ask them, they will readily explain that the pike keeps himself busy trying to catch the carp, and they both fidget uneasily and turn around every now and again. This causes the Earth to rotate. As for the right-eyed flounder resembling a flat tin Moon, he provides lighting for these activities and meditates upon the meaning of time, bodily movements and vain fishy desires.

Writ in Water

Scylla was once smitten with Charybdis, and Master Builder erected a pile-up house for them. It is under new ownership now, and crumbles around those who inhabit it. The Gulf Stream still runs through it.

At high tide, waves rock this fortress of discontent, striving to establish the Law of the Abyss instead of the Law of the Shallows. Some odd creatures bubble and belly out at the very surface of sense, many of them two-headed, others lacking a dorsal fin. Who they are or whether they have names remains unknown. Reportedly, one of them once introduced himself as Mr. Party.

Quests and Discoveries

It was the epoch of great underwater discoveries. All the ships were diverting their routes into the blue deep. After trawling the sea-bed, scientists on board the repaired *Titanic* found deposits of copper and silver. Before long, multitudes plunged into the depths, searching for gold they had glimpsed in brilliant sunlit flashes. This was where our mutual ancestor, the Great Hero of the West, met a wonderful Eskimo girl wearing a fur coat and short doeskin boots. She had just run out of oxygen, which proved to be an excellent reason for striking up an acquaintance.

The Border Mouse

He circumnavigates no man's land like a neurotic sun. If a boundary-line is drawn across a river, he is a fish; if it cuts through a bog, he turns into a frog, a bully-belly, languishing red eyes. He is the storm of the moment, a mole gnawing at the roots of trust.

When the day is young, he smells seeds of darkness and poppy lips, sunburst oranges and crimson lava out of the mouth of rage. He smells the ever-widening crevices of Europe, and he smells the time when he'll unhide himself. When money blossoms, he smells it.

An artist of nuisance, he suddenly paints himself into our peripheral vision. He is the rust-colored evening of our lives. History won't expose his worn-out shadow: it disregards its margins and has no imagination.

Making room for empty spaces—or unmarked graves—is easy. An infinity mirror holds us all. Nothingness, like greatness, emerges from a mouse hole of eternity.

Pseudoaluminum and the Big Plans

The bigger the house, the smaller the occupants. The same goes for the devil: in huts, he used to oust the inhabitants, while in skyscrapers he can humble himself into a snuff-box.

The devil gradually loses prestige. His dung, however, still ornaments the fields. They send students to investigate this red clay. They hope it contains plenty of pseudoaluminum, the raw material of super-high-speed bombers and portrait frames.

Cause and Effect

Anton van Leeuwenhoek made a spyglass that allowed viewers to observe the past. In that past, dinosaurs put in an appearance, and also fleas as big as mammoths. There were scores of them, so each time Leeuwenhoek withdrew the spyglass fearfully from his eye.

Having calmed himself down with a glass of ginger beer, Leeuwenhoek would go out of doors. He halted somewhere in a small park, placed his hand on the trunk of a tree, and waited patiently until an ant or a beetle climbed onto the back of it. "Tiny, they are still tiny," Leeuwenhoek whispered, in a moment of mental aberration confusing the past with the future and the cause with the effect.

Oasis

The demon of ready-made things erects Potemkin villages and other monuments to deception. The ghost named Torricelli busies himself with inflating mirages of culture. The imp called Do It Yourself ornaments a typical Kara-Kum landscape with small green bushes. In the evenings, the three of them watch gray flowers of decay open into a colorless twilight and hiss their whispers into travelers' ears: "If you're invited to an oasis, you surely are in a desert."

Watch How This Picture
Paints Another Picture

The Fifth International of honest people is dressed in words. Shielded by timeproof and breathable books, its members dwell in the thicket of their breath. They can't tell their inside from the outside.

What they use for maps the others unmap. Hiding behind brimstone billows of pragma, they watch clay doves fly to the top of a fancy. They can open doors with their bare smiles.

At the table, they talk about dark-skinned practice targets maimed by droppings of a high-flying delusion. Their knowledge is sand-colored and grainy; it can be shaped into their next steps across the finitude of their pasteboard boxes.

Grandeur Way

More winters or just this one.
—Horace

The Hydra-headed father of the nation looks like the day you meet him. He is sick to his lobbies; his airports swell but he'll survive a bout of motleyness.

He uncled many nomads and expellees who disguise their true navels with raggery. His second ugliest head is heavy-jawed about it.

According to *The Hades News,* he has inherited a little acre in Tartarus. This gives him a hellish pleasure, but, due to being immortal, he may find claiming his fortune problematic. Still, history keeps trying until it succeeds.

Anatoly Kudryavitsky

An Unfriendly Gesture

Lined up on the shelf, there they were, participants in the looming war of people against their household appliances: battle cruisers of steam irons, forts of teapots, flame-throwers of vacuum cleaners. All this stuff had been supplied by a bunch of baddies, who knew perfectly well that size doesn't matter at all and that man can make a galosh as big as the *Titanic* and then put his foot into it.

A Pacification Meeting of the Clocks

A professor of poetry and a drifter poet row a tandem kayak together through the crimson decline of customary meanings. Their watches show different predicaments, their names also denote disunity. Above them, a rusty cloud of mutual mistrust.

Velvety waves bloom; the hats ooze memories. Listen to the hands speak:

"Why us, Lord?"

"Why not?"

Rocks rise as the moon recedes. The Milky Way of civilisation remains uncharted.

Anatoly Kudryavitsky

Pastures of Elderly Men

A leafy sheen of sunlight speaks to silence in its own language. Exposed to a hypothetical counting eye in the sky, sheep twenty-two and sheep twenty-three show off the red numbers on their backs.

In shed-like houses, human spare parts are gradually fading into rust. Fungus-impregnated walls reminisce about the olden days of barn dancing when the earth would call to sky hornpipes for a tune.

No couples are up for a dance these days. "Women don't survive here," a woman of eighty whispers.

Taking Care

In the entanglement of human trees, both cryptogams and phanerogams, each branch outlines a face. A local Save the Grove group is active here; the volunteers have entrenched themselves in an elevated state of mind.

Small talk wafts over from the tents on the smell of curry reaching for the thirst-colored sky. While the roots snake their way to puddles of alphabet tincture, some leaves manage to break free—with or without an inscription.

End of the Beginning

As reality is pregnant with Chaos, we rejoice at having children who can crack any code, but they instantly forget what they've deciphered. The codes give obedience the slip and lay themselves out like written scrolls, replacing the carpets and rivers, percolating under the doors.

It's all in vain: the secrets of the ages no longer interest anyone. Life has become unwritten, and Logos has been separated from Ethos and Pathos. While the sun draws book-shaped rectangles on the walls, the air gets littered with important words.

Out of the deep indigo, Chaos finally comes to be; Aion holds it in his arms. The sleeves of time smell of dampness.

Part IV.
Interesting Times

Chamber Music

Maturity comes with a punnet of golden plums. It says, refrain from eating the fruit.

Inside my room there's another, an invisible one. As the day sheds its colors, the plums too become indiscernible. And I am beginning to resemble an old plum tree; its leaves rustle as I breathe.

Altius

It was the day the sky adopted the clarity of evening thoughts. On the seashore, lit by the setting sun, there was a statue of a man with his arm raised heavenward. Someone put a bottle in the man's hand, and it shone like the ultimate desire.

When I next saw the statue, the bottle wasn't there. The hand was also missing. But the statue was still pointing at the celestial heights, this time with the empty sleeve.

Out of Harm's Way

in memoriam Daniel Harms, the Russian absurdist writer

Motorists own imaginary and non-existent things, such as distances and remote countries. Stepping on the accelerator, they hasten the pace of a clock, but time has to wait for slumbrous planes pausing in the clouds.

Pedestrians own meadows and riverbanks. Dawn and twilight mix colors for them; the whole horizon encircles their eyeballs.

Here, amidst the monotony of some German town, time splits into grains of memory and I plunge into the quicksands of *déjà vu*. It seems to me that I am treading the streets of quite another German town. The day has hidden its colors, frames of a static theatre mist up and everything fades into gray, comes to a halt. Madness is never far away....

In the following moment, the sticky haze disgorges a signboard: "HARMS, THE FIXER. CALL ME ON 92 27 11." I ponder on the multitude of towns and countries plagued with absurdity—and there aren't a lot of such signs around!

Then the roaring of a motor pushes slightly the frozen minute-hand.

Dialogue with the Sphinx

The sphinx was studying the fractal frame of sunbeams reflected off the nearby pyramid, not paying any attention to the professor's touristy outfit.

The professor was thinking of saying something like "Nice day today, isn't it?" but instead uttered hesitatingly, "Fear me not; I am Man, King of Nature."

Maybe it wasn't the worst way of winning the sphinx's attention because his neck creaked a little—and the professor heard a centuries-old voice saying:

"You … Yes, you. The one that's staring at me. What do you see?"

"A human face," the Professor replied trying not to look at his saddle-nose.

"Start walking around me. What do you see now?"

"Wings of an eagle."

"Take a few more steps."

"Lion's paws."

"… and another couple of steps."

"Tail of an ox."

"Now go back to the starting point."

"That face again."

"So what do you think you've been looking at?"

The professor remembered the fate of those who failed the sphinx's challenge, and so took his time before answering cautiously: "Nothing but myself."

The sphinx smiled in a scornful way, and regained stiffness.

Games Pebbles Play

In the eternity before this eternity, all the being was rust-colored. Pebbles on the seashore, naked and identical, evolved to play apes.

"How did apekind's history begin?" "From an idea of ape." "How did the idea of ape begin?" "From an idea of ape god." "Should we accept this idea?"

Lo, pebbles on the shore playing apes.

"What is this ape god?" "Let us say, the biggest stone." "We all seem to be identical." "That is the one on which we are lying." "So ape god is the ground of Being. We accept the idea of ape god."

Naked pebbles on the shore playing games. Playing apes.

"We have no history." "Nor do we have a clue." "What do we have?" "Caressing waves. Salt in the wind. An infinity ahead of us." "Is that enough?"

The everlasting night was saturated with destiny. Apes had no time for pebbles since they were busy learning to use bigger, pointed stones.

Anatoly Kudryavitsky

Non-Yielding Darkness

On man's right side an angel abides, and on the left side, Satan. The latter is married to a life-size Marilyn Monroe doll (pure silicone, pinchable.) A couple of drowned girls provide more punchable entertainment for him. Once in a while, in a fit of jealousy, they cast a spell against dolls, to no purpose. The devil's Facebook timeline gets littered with bad omens and other phenomena. Dwelling in a haremized space, he finds it hard to keep pace with daily developments, so life, at his request, decelerates. "Time is hard to visualize"—say the doll's eyes. But even if life comes to a halt, the devil will surely stick to his weatherworn and very human habit of making statements on behalf of the nameless and the deceased.

Reinforcing the Trap

Our past is our namesake; our future, someone nameless. Recipes for disaster make a good read.

Leather sofas rush into position: the show is on, martyrs of evolution traipse from Nowhere to Erewhon: a millipede, a dinosaur, and an anthropoid ape.

Behind them, dark memory gaps; awaiting them, kisses of darkness.

At their feet, the river they can't step into twice; ahead of them, an unfordable ford.

To the south of them, gasps of nightly death; to the north, the death of night.

Anatoly Kudryavitsky

Lost in Međimurje

for Dražen Katunarić

On a day without a number in the month of *listopad* the wind of amnesia sweeps the red roofs. An ancient mound crowned with new grass fades into its withered memories. Autumn hasn't yet drowned in winter, and the path to the pastures of the past leads to the candlelit windows into perseverance. Cinderella dances there with a wooden Marie Corelli; three daughters of success unword the story of their porcelain marriage to Mr. Nutcracker. The future gets littered with things from bygone dreams. "If there is a future," the field croons its mud song. The tree growing inside a ruined house keeps vigil over the waters of chaos.

The Mother of All Parades

As the empire exhales the dust of its former glory, you merge into a vast mutual body with multiple pebble heads. Cigarette smoke searches pockets and lungs.

If you doze off now, you'll see skeletons marching past through Red Square and rockets watching them closely from the rostra.

When you open your eyes again, festivities will go on. You'll still have a chance to observe the huge inflated faces rising into the air.

Journey to the Infinite

In Belarus, you travel along pulsating paths under the sky sores and cloud curves. Out of the future's gap-tooth grin comes a motorway poster: *STOP! SHOOT A WOLF!*

There are no wolves in sight. Your alertness breathes in the language of landing snowflakes. Silence is the troubled outskirts of the city of sounds.

STOP! SHOOT A WOLF!

Who ever carries a gun? Who can shoot well enough? Who knows that the moment of relief is the moment of undoing?

STOP! SHOOT A WOLF!

And you begin to think over a practical solution to the task you face.

Teddy Bear and a Russian Toy

"I may be perceived as a softie, but I am a creature of principle," Teddy Bear growled. "What about you—have *you* got a squeaky thing inside?"

Vanka-Vstanka, a tilting doll, rattled: "What for, my dear chap? What for? My center of gravity lies below my belt, so I'll straighten up with a smile every time I get bear-handled."

"Now tell me the secret, you phallic keeper of verticality, you tireless Russky burden-bearer," Teddy Bear snarled. "Tell me, are they real, your blue eyes, baby face, and crimson blush?"

"No, they are limned," the Russian toy tilted. "But look at this paint—it doesn't peel, you know."

Repossession

I am a two-bedroom house exploring life after death, committing adultery with a new occupier. Somebody presently possesses the silence of my books and the tenderness of my home-grown lemons, but the duty of owning is not the same as the art of knowing.

My windows used to glass off the passing of ancient constellations; today they grimace at machine-washed ideas on the line. Family warmth leaks from the pipes into the garden of trimmed expectations.

The dark-time television is a flood. Something surfaces: an eternity behind, an eternity ahead, and the soundless mouse-running of an imperceptible "now."

Irregular History

According to the Irregular History textbook, the Napoleonic Wars began in 1933 and Pearl Harbor was bombed in 1984. Genghis Khan was really a Przhevalski's horse; Aesop, Morse code; and Herostratus, the Statue of Liberty. Moreover, they all were alive only twenty years ago.

Sitting on the bank of eternity, I visualize history rewriting and broadcasting itself. Of course, it can get a little condensed at times, but in a couple of millennia will this even count as irregular?

Anatoly Kudryavitsky

Structuralism: An Assay

Water can be separated into oxygen and hydrogen. A man decomposes into the skeleton and other people's memories. An empire splits into nostalgia and a common language.

But a stone breaks up into stones.

Part V.
From
"An Uneasy Habitat"

Versions by Carol Rumens

Letters from the Afterlife

When the letters from the afterlife finally reached us, we found out at last who is doing what. Shakespeare is working on a play called *Joseph Stalin,* Bach is writing a cantata on the German unification, Leo Tolstoy, who has converted to Islam, prays a lot and goes by the name of Muhammed Abdulla, Van Gogh has sunk into black melancholy and does no work at all because he needs nature and bright colors, whereas only transparent cloaks are available—myriads of transparent cloaks, the color of autumn air.

Anatoly Kudryavitsky

The Two-Headed Man and the Paper Life

There was once a two-headed man. He sat at an office desk and wrote down somebody's fate. Employees went to and fro carrying folders full of everyday-ness. Peeping in, a little girl shuddered with convulsions, and shrieked, "What's this HORRIBLE THING doing here?"

The girl was taken away and treated for hallucinations; guards were stationed at the doors.

This tale is told merely for the edification of those who enjoy peeping through the keyholes of their paper lives.

The Center of the Universe

The red comb of that pheasant is the center of the universe. The pheasant moves and sometimes even flies, and the center of the universe shifts about with him. Why this particular pheasant, you ask, and why his comb? But the One Who Knows The Answers has already shrugged his shoulders, the movement causing his gray comb to shake at the same time.

Anatoly Kudryavitsky

Be Careful with Kites

When flying a kite in the long-suffering heavens, you never know what you may catch. If it's a dead bird or a piece of aircraft metal, no problem. But supposing a snag gets caught, or, God forbid, the moon? Our daring kite-flier will then find himself in direct and prolonged connection with the skies.

And it isn't so far the case that, should he finally decide to release the kite, it won't give chase to him.

Hearts

A person contains many different hearts. The forehead-heart is marble, and never crumbles, unlike the back-of-the-head heart, which is made of quartz. The heart of the jugular fossa is made of wood, well polished by the blood-stream. The celluloid stomach-heart was digested a long time ago. In addition, there is the heart of the private parts and the heart of the heel, but the first is not studied, because it hides somewhere in the mediastinum, and the second is easily perceived while walking through life's jungles. They say that a heart-heart has also been discovered inside somebody—but it's better not to lift the lid on this mystery.

007

James Bond retired and settled in the Soviet Union—for whose break-up he was responsible. His pension was delivered to him by pigeon-post from Yorkshire. On Tuesdays, the former 007 attended party members' meetings, and made recordings with a tape-recorder embedded in a cigarette. The meetings ended with the singing of the *Internationale* but James Bond, on principle, murmured through his gray mustache, "God Save the Queen." "Here's our comrade from the developing republics singing out of tune," said the nimble old men, in their Pioneer ties, patting Bond lovingly on his cast-iron shoulders.

In a Chink in the Void

In a chink in the void, blows on the top of the head by a porcelain god were introduced as a means of persuasion. Persuaded people silently endured, and realized the depths of their delusions. God silently endured, thinking that when somebody needed to be punished, the one that got punished was always himself.

Anatoly Kudryavitsky

Aesthetics

At first, the Montagues and Capulets were friends. But then there arose a disagreement concerning the style of their hats. When aesthetics are involved, mountains of dead bodies will follow without fail.

Friendship till Death

It's difficult to be on friendly terms with your friends. All could be well, were it not for their nice habit of working with scissors.

"More tea?" my friend asks kindly, trimming my left ear. "Some vodka perhaps?" the other friend adds, simultaneously cutting off my surplus chin.

Crawling away, completely bandaged, I take to my bed at an unknown enemy's place, and when people approach me I make a hideous animal face, so as not to tempt them to sudden friendship.

Letters

The letters that contain the warmth of a hand come through the main entrance and rest for a long time in an armchair, watching how the outgoing answer arrays itself in a macintosh.

The letters containing the warmth of a heart knock uselessly at the back entrance and may sometimes be sniffed out by dogs and devoured by rats.

For letters with hearts enclosed, a fairly large rubbish-bin, placed on the distant approaches to the house, readies its jaws.

Electric Shavers

Electric shavers work by night: you can see the lawn has been cut, your neighbor's thoughts have somehow been evened up, and the hill on the horizon has disappeared somewhere. In the morning, the shavers are telling us something, but we fail to understand their agitated buzz.

Anatoly Kudryavitsky

Inspiration

Aesop liked tinkling his collar bells—it was an excellent way to nod off. Many times his master tried to exchange the useless old man for some nice-looking young slave-girl, but the only offer he received was a broken plow and a couple of cart-wheels. Whenever the master took one of the slave-girls to bed, his parrot began to express its feelings by talking in parables. Aesop would sneak up with his stylus and start to make notes. Deprived of their share of love, the slave-girls turned the old man out, but he kept on coming back, muttering something.

Pressed Down by a Book

Early, or even earlier, the desk encyclopaedia approaches you and asks the sacred question: "How do you wish to live, so that you can be included in me, or so that I, with all my content, can be placed inside you?"

No answer guarantees anything, except the chance to spend your life in the black-and-white dream instead of the colored one. Thus books take their quiet revenge on people.

The Alarm-Clock Bomb

The alarm-clock bomb rings up like an uninvited guest and offers you an experience of ravaged Nirvana. There's nothing you can do except sing it the pointless song, "May there always be me." Sometimes the alarm-clock looms up first, quietly ticking in the doorway. It's better that you hear it.

ACKNOWLEDGMENTS

Grateful acknowledgment is made to the editors of the following, in which a number of these poems, or versions of them, originally appeared:

The American Journal of Poetry: "Lost in Međimurje" and "Repossession"

Das Gedicht: "Altius" and "Sex Toy Mistaken for an Angel"

The Honest Ulsterman: "The Border Mouse"

Ink, Sweat & Tears: "The Sky in Their Eyes"

*Ken*again:* "Games Pebbles Play"

Landing Places, eds. Eva Bourke & Borbála Faragó (Dedalus Press, 2010): "Teddy Bear and a Russian Toy" and "Out of Harm's Way"

Matter: "The Wind of History"

A Night in the Nabokov Hotel, ed. Anatoly Kudryavitsky (Dedalus Press, 2006): "Pseudoaluminium and the Big Plans"

Otoliths: "Watch How This Picture Paints Another Picture"

Plume: "Somewhere in Eastern Europe"

Revival: "Structuralism: An Assay"

The SHOp: "Hunting in a Flagged Zone" and "Writ in Water"

Shot Glass Journal: "Gravitation," "Oasis," "The Three Fishes Theory," "Grandeur Way," "Cause and Effect," and "The Mother of All Parades"

Stride: "In a Whale's Belly," "British Lions," "The Worm of Doubt," "The Book of Meros," and "A Promenade"

Sulphur: "Taking Care"

Under the Radar: "Pabako"

Carol Rumens' translations of "Letters from the Afterlife" and "Pressed Down by a Book" first appeared in *Oxford Poetry;* her translation of "Friendship till Death," in *The Liberal,* and her translation of "In a Chink of the Void," in *Four Centuries.* Her versions of "The Two-Headed Man and the Paper Life," "The Center of the Universe," "Be Careful with Kites," "007," "Aesthetics," and "The Alarm-Clock Bomb" first appeared in her collection of poems *Blind Spots* (Seren, Wales, 2008.)

About the Author

Anatoly Kudryavitsky is a Moscow-born Irish poet and novelist of Polish/Irish descent, the grandson of an Irishman who ended up in Stalin's Gulag. A holder of a PhD from Moscow Medical Academy, he has a background in biology, Celtic heritage, music and literature, and worked as a researcher, a journalist, a literary translator, and a magazine editor. He started writing poetry in the 1980s, but under the Communists was not permitted to publish his work openly—until the years of Perestroika. In 1989, his poems and stories first appeared in magazines. He is the former writer-in-residence for the State Literary Museum of Russia. Having emigrated in 1999, he has since been living in Dublin, Ireland. Between 2006 and 2009 he worked as a creative writing tutor for the Irish Writers' Centre. He is a bilingual author writing in English and Russian, and has published a collection of his English poems, *Shadow of Time* (Goldsmith Press, Ireland, 2005) and three collections of his haiku, the latest being *Horizon* (Red Moon Press, USA, 2016), as well as seven collections of his Russian poems, the latest title being *Selected Prose Poems* (Evgeny Stepanov Press, Moscow, 2017). The English translation of his latest novel appeared as *The Flying Dutchman* (Glagoslav, UK, 2018). He edited two anthologies of haiku from Ireland, *Bamboo Dreams* (Doghouse Books, 2012) and *Between the Leaves* (Arlen House, 2016), and also edited and translated into English four anthologies of contemporary Russian, Ukrainian, and German poetry published by Dedalus Press and Glagoslav. In 2003, he won the Maria Edgeworth Poetry Prize (Ireland), and in 2017 was the recipient of the Mihai Eminescu Academy Poetry Award (Romania). His works have been translated into fourteen languages. He lives in Dublin, Ireland, and edits *SurVision* poetry magazine.